FAURE
Fantasie

for flute and piano

Editor: Trevor Wye

Chester Music

(A Music Sales Limited Company)

8/9 Frith Street, London, W1V 5TZ

Exclusive distributors: Music Sales Ltd., Newmarket Road,
Bury St. Edmunds, Suffolk, IP33 3YB.

EDITOR'S NOTE

GABRIEL FAURE (1845 - 1924)

Fauré, born in Ariège, France, studied with Saint-Saens. His genius was largely unrecognised during his lifetime perhaps because his music is discreet and subtle, and many people in France at this time refused to believe in a composer who had written no operas.

It was in 1898, the same year that he visited London, that Fauré wrote his Fantasie which he dedicated to Paul Taffanel. Flute players are indeed fortunate that out of a handful of miniatures which he wrote for one instrument and piano, Fauré has given us this gem.

à Paul Taffanel
Fantasie
for Flute and Piano

Edited by Trevor Wye

GABRIEL FAURE
Op. 79

6

7

SELECTED MUSIC FOR FLUTE AND KEYBOARD

J. C. BACH	Sonata Op.18 No.1
J. S. BACH	Book 1: Sonatas Nos. 1-3
J. S. BACH	Book 2: Sonatas Nos. 4-6
BENTZON	Variations on an Original Theme
BERKELEY	Concerto (with Piano Reduction)
BERKELEY	Sonata
COOPER	Sonata for Flutes
DOPPLER	Hungarian Pastoral Fantasy Op.26
FAURE	Fantasie Op.79
FAURE	Sicilienne
LE FLEMING	Air and Dance
GENIN	Carnival of Venice Op.14
GODARD	Suite de Trois Morceaux
HOVLAND	Suite
B. KELLY	Sonatina
KREBS	Sonata in A Major
KVANDAL	Romance
MACONCHY	Colloquy
MAW	Sonatina
NIELSEN	The Fog is Lifting
POULENC	Sonata
SCOTT	Scotch Pastoral
STANLEY	Six Solos Op.4
TELEMANN	Sonata in B Minor
VIVALDI	Sonata in C

SOLO FLUTE

BENTZON	Variations Op.93
BERGE	Flute Solo
DEBUSSY	Syrinx
MORTENSEN	Sonata Op.6
NIELSEN	The Children are Playing
SOMMERFELDT	Divertimento
WESTERGAARD	Sonata

STUDIES

ANDERSEN	24 Short Studies Op. 33
ANDERSEN	100 Posthumous Studies
ANDERSEN	26 Small Caprices Op. 37
ANDERSEN	24 Technical Studies Op. 63
BOEHM	24 Capriccios
KÖHLER	Progress in Flute Playing Book 1 Op. 33
KÖHLER	Progress in Flute Playing Book 2 Op. 33
KÖHLER	Progress in Flute Playing Book 3 Op. 33

From

Chester Music

(A Music Sales Limited Company)
8/9 Frith Street, London, W1V 5TZ
Exclusive distributors: Music Sales Ltd., Newmarket Road,
Bury St. Edmunds, Suffolk, IP33 3YB.

FAURE
Fantasie
for flute and piano

Editor: Trevor Wye

Chester Music
(A Music Sales Limited Company)
8/9 Frith Street, London, W1V 5TZ
Exclusive distributors: Music Sales Ltd., Newmarket Road,
Bury St. Edmunds, Suffolk, IP33 3YB.

à Paul Taffanel

Fantasie
for Flute and Piano

Edited by Trevor Wye

GABRIEL FAURE
Op. 79

4

6

14

16

Printed by Halstan & Co. Ltd., Amersham, Bucks., England

Mixed Bag

WOODWIND ENSEMBLE

A series which offers
MAXIMUM FLEXIBILITY
in relation to

* students' varied
  technical abilities
* instrumentation
* number of players
* range of music

1. TCHAIKOVSKY Waltz of the Flowers
2. THE FIVE CHORD TRICK (Graham Lyons)
   A Composition in the 'Rock' Idiom
3. PURCELL'S POPULAR PIECES
   Rondeau from Adbelazer - Air in D minor -
   Trumpet Tune
4. HAYDN Sonatina in G
5. TWO JOPLIN RAGS
   The Entertainer - Ragtime Dance
6. CHRISTMAS CAROL SUITE
   The Holly and the Ivy - Away in a Manger -
   The Coventry Carol - Unto us a Boy is Born
7. BIZET Suite from L'Arlésienne
8. GRIEG Suite from Peer Gynt
9. BEETHOVEN SUITE
   Fur Elise - Minuet in G - Ode to Joy
10. MOZART
    Minuet in G minor (Symphony No. 40)
11. MUSIC AT THE COURT OF HENRY VIII
    Helas Madame - Blow Thy Horn, Hunter -
    En Vray Amoure - Consort IX -
    Hey Trolly Lolly Lo!
12. MIXED BAG OF BOOGIE (Graham Lyons)
13. THREE MINIATURES (Rory Boyle)
14. HAYDN Three Pieces for Mechanical Clock
15. SCHUBERT Three Dances
16. THE ASH GROVE - The Miller of Dee -
    A-Roving
17. J. S. BACH Sheep May Safely Graze
18. SMOKEY JOE (Karl Jenkins)
    Blue Waltz - Those Old Twelve-Bar Blues -
    Shufflin'
19. BOCCHERINI Minuet and Trio
20. HANDEL The Water Music (selection)
21. CUMBRIA (John Cameron)
    Grasmere - Castlerigg - Daffodils
    The Hawkshead Stage
22. WIEN! (Graham Lyons)
    A Waltz in the style of Old Vienna
23. MOZART MIX
    Three Easy Pieces by Mozart
24. SHOSTAKOVICH
    March - Waltz - The Bear
25. ELGAR Chanson de Matin
26. ELGAR Land of Hope and Glory
    (Two themes from Pomp and Circumstance)
27. COME DANCING (Karl Jenkins)
    Foxy Trot - Tango Time - Wendy's
    Waltz - Rumbastious
28. MONTEVERDI Toccata
    (Three pieces from the operas)
29. MUSIC FOR A WESTERN
    (Rory Boyle)
30. HULLABALOOBELAY!
    Hornpipe and other sea songs

ENSEMBLES POUR BOIS

Une série offrant un
**MAXIMUM DE CHOIX D'ADAP-
TATIONS** en fonction des

* divers aptitudes
  techniques des étudiants
* de l'instrumentation
* du nombre d'exécutants
* de la musique choisie

HOLZBLÄSER ENSEMBLES

Eine Reihe mit
**GRÖSSTER VARIATIONS-
BREITE** in bezug auf

* den unterschiedlichen
  Standard der Schüler
* die instrumentation
* die Anzahl der Spieler
* die Auswahl an Musik

CONJUNTOS DE VIENTO

Una colección que ofrece
MAXIMA FLEXIBILIDAD
en cuanto a:

* estudiantes de diferentes
  grados de experiencia
* instrumentación
* número de instrumentistas
* repertorio musical

木管アンサンブル

このシリーズは
以下の様な目的のために
最大限の適応性をもっている:

★生徒の様々な
　技量に応じて
★楽器編成に応じて
★演奏者の数に応じて
★豊富なレパートリとして

Chester Music

(A Music Sales Limited Company)
8/9 Frith Street, London, W1V 5TZ
Exclusive distributors: Music Sales Ltd., Newmarket Road,
Bury St. Edmunds, Suffolk, IP33 3YB.

SELECTED MUSIC FOR FLUTE AND KEYBOARD

J. C. BACH	Sonata Op.18 No.1
J. S. BACH	Book 1: Sonatas Nos. 1-3
J. S. BACH	Book 2: Sonatas Nos. 4-6
BENTZON	Variations on an Original Theme
BERKELEY	Concerto (with Piano Reduction)
BERKELEY	Sonata
COOPER	Sonata for Flutes
DOPPLER	Hungarian Pastoral Fantasy Op.26
FAURE	Fantasie Op.79
FAURE	Sicilienne
LE FLEMING	Air and Dance
GENIN	Carnival of Venice Op.14
GODARD	Suite de Trois Morceaux
HOVLAND	Suite
B. KELLY	Sonatina
KREBS	Sonata in A Major
KVANDAL	Romance
MACONCHY	Colloquy
MAW	Sonatina
NIELSEN	The Fog is Lifting
POULENC	Sonata
SCOTT	Scotch Pastoral
STANLEY	Six Solos Op.4
TELEMANN	Sonata in B Minor
VIVALDI	Sonata in C

SOLO FLUTE

BENTZON	Variations Op.93
BERGE	Flute Solo
DEBUSSY	Syrinx
MORTENSEN	Sonata Op.6
NIELSEN	The Children are Playing
SOMMERFELDT	Divertimento
WESTERGAARD	Sonata

STUDIES

ANDERSEN	24 Short Studies Op. 33
ANDERSEN	100 Posthumous Studies
ANDERSEN	26 Small Caprices Op. 37
ANDERSEN	24 Technical Studies Op. 63
BOEHM	24 Capriccios
KÖHLER	Progress in Flute Playing Book 1 Op. 33
KÖHLER	Progress in Flute Playing Book 2 Op. 33
KÖHLER	Progress in Flute Playing Book 3 Op. 33

From

Chester Music
(A Music Sales Limited Company)
8/9 Frith Street, London, W1V 5TZ
Exclusive distributors: Music Sales Ltd., Newmarket Road,
Bury St. Edmunds, Suffolk, IP33 3YB.

Flute   Editor: Trevor Wye   Clarinet   Editor: Thea King

Oboe   Editor: James Brown   Bassoon   Editor: William Waterhouse

Saxophone   Editor: Paul Harvey

A growing collection of volumes from Chester Music, containing a
wide range of pieces from different periods.

FLUTE SOLOS VOLUME I

Baston	Siciliana from Concertino in D
Blavet	Gavotte—La Dédale
Bochsa	Nocturne
Buchner	Russian Melody from Fantasy op. 22
Eichner	Minuet from Sonata No. 6
Franck	Intrada
Franck	Galliard
Lichtenthal	Theme
Mozart	Minuets I & II from Sonata No. 1
Paisiello	Nel Cor Più
Vivaldi	Andante from Sonata No. 3 of The Faithful Shepherd
Vivaldi	Pastorale from Sonata No. 4 of The Faithful Shepherd

FLUTE SOLOS VOLUME II

Blavet	Les Tendres Badinages from Sonata No. 6
Chopin	A Rossini Theme
Donjon	Adagio Nobile
Eichner	Scherzando from Sonata No. 6
Harmston	Andante
Jacob	Cradle Song from Five Pieces for Harmonica and Piano
Mozart	Minuets I & II from Sonata No. 5
Mozart	Allegro from Sonata in G
Pauli	Capriccio
Telemann	Tempo Giusto from Sonata in D minor
Vivaldi	Allegro from Sonata No. 6 of The Faithful Shepherd

FLUTE SOLOS VOLUME III

Blavet	Sicilienne from Sonata No. 4
Blavet	Les Regrets from Sonata No. 5
Donjon	Offertoire op. 12
Eichner	Allegro from Sonata No. 6
Kelly	Jig from Serenade
Loeillet	Gavotte and Aria from Sonata No. 7
Nørgard	Andantino—Pastorale
Sibelius	Solo from Scaramouche op. 71
Telemann	Grave from Sonata in G minor
Vivaldi	Largo from Sonata No. 6 of The Faithful Shepherd

Also available: FLUTE DUETS AND TRIOS
Further details on request

Chester Music

(A Music Sales Limited Company)
8/9 Frith Street, London, W1V 5TZ
Exclusive distributors: Music Sales Ltd., Newmarket Road,
Bury St. Edmunds, Suffolk, IP33 3YB.